Kid Pomes

Brian Leo

Illustrated by Lanessa Miller

Author's Tranquility Press

MARRIETA, GEORGIA

Brian Leo /Author's Tranquility Press
2706 Station Club Drive SW
Marietta, GA 30060
www.authorstranquilitypress.com

Ordering Information:
Quantity sales. Special discounts are available on quantity purchases by corporations, associations, and others. For details, contact the "Special Sales Department" at the address above.

Kid Pomes / Brian Leo 1st Edition 2018, 2nd Edition 2022
Paperback: 978-1-958179-42-0
eBook: 978-1-958179-43-7

Notes from the author

This started out as an exercise. I was teaching theatrical improvisation to some fifth and sixth graders at my wife's school, and we needed something for the kids to do for the concluding parents' night. I wasn't sure they were ready to do cold improv after only six weeks or so of training, so I had them recite some silly poems by Shel Silverstein. That was fine the first year, even the second, but by the third we needed something new. I decided to write my own, and these became the School Life poems in this book.

Then my youngest granddaughter came along. Among the games we played was a lot of silliness, and I began to write the Home Life poems for her. In time I wanted to share these with other peoples' kids but I needed an illustrator.

I've worked for many years as an entertainer in the Renaissance Faire circuit, under the name Tinker MacLea, and it was at one of the faires that I met Lanessa Miller. Though she usually draws excellent, lifelike portraits, she agreed to work on my whimsical project, and a book was born.

We hope you will read this with and to some kids you love. God bless!

B. Leo
Frankfort, IL
December, 2018

"For Alanna, of course..."

Contents

The Home Life Poems...I

Afraid 73

Allowance 43

Baby 7

Bicycle 53

Birthday 69

Bob 15

Boom...89

Breakfast...9

Brown and Blue 67

Burned 45

Candy Plan..75

Car 95

Cleaning 57

Creativity 41

Dark...47

Death 91

Dinner..29

Donuts 17

Downscaling 61

Driver...39

Gift...11

Good Night...37

Kids 19

The Know-It-All 21

The Last 55

Lawn 81

Music 13

Pets 59

Polite 77

Present 33

Recycled 25

Runaway 87

Shirt 23

Shoveling 5

Shower 71

Skeeters 31

Smile 63

Spider 83

Stuffed 27

Sweet Tooth 93

Tables 65

Tears 85

Thief 49

TV 3

Tree 51

Window 935

Worry 79

The School Life Poems 97

Aardvark 139

Alarming 137

Allegiance 113

Answer 115

Baloney and Cheese 125

Belief 153

Detention 147

Find X 117

Historical First 145

Independent Thought 131

In Line 121

Johnny Quiller 107

Late 123

Lonely 161

The Loop 143

Lost 155

Love 111

My Locker 101

Names 105

Principal 133

Rain 119

Report Card 159

Rope Climber 127

Small 149

The Substitute 103

Super Student 141

Sweet 135

To the Point 109

Traded 157

Welcome 99

Yay! 151

THE FINALE 163

The Home
Life Poems

TV

We did all our chores, so she said I could watch
the TV with my kid brother Sean.
So we watched it for hours.
Maybe next time she'll let us
both watch it AND turn the thing on.

Shoveling

I do not mind shoveling snow.
Though it's cold out, I never complain.
But I'm tired of the kids who all mock me and laugh
when I'm sent out to shovel the rain.

Baby

Mom says she wants a new baby
'cause she misses the one she once had.
In all my four years, there's been none around here.
No baby, just Mom, me and Dad.
But I've seen baby clothes in stored boxes,
and some photos of a baby in frames.
So, yes, I am getting suspicious;
I don't like it when grown-ups play games.
If this family once had a baby,
where is it? Are they pulling a fast one?
And I'm not eating anything Mama may cook
till I know what they did with their last one.

Breakfast

I promised to make my Mom breakfast in bed,
with eggs, bacon, juice and some toast.
So her favorite jam I spread onto some bread,
which I stuck in the oven to roast.
In the door of the fridge was a bottle of juice
labeled "lemon," so I poured a big cup.
And I couldn't find the bacon, but that's no excuse;
sticks of gum look the same all fried up.
But when eggs in the toaster refused to cook right,
I remembered that boiled ones pleased her.
So I fried up some water and cooked her my best:
the marshmallow ones from last Easter!

Gift

I wrote and wrote to Santa, begging,
"Bring me a guitar,"
and on Christmas Eve, guess what?
That's what he brings!
But I should have made it clearer.
He's an older guy, y'know.
I meant the kind that also comes with strings.

Music

When I practice clarinet, it isn't pretty.
I can hear dogs howling all across the city.
But although I'm told the noise turns bricks to powder,
if it bugs my sister, I'll keep playing louder.

Bob

I was named for my dear old great-grandpa,
Jubilation Methuselah Cobb.
But I'd like to survive on the playground,
so I tell all the kids my name's Bob.

Donuts

Enough with the broccoli, cabbage and beets!
Our garden should grow things a real kid eats.
Enough with tomatoes, potatoes and beans!
The same for that lettuce and all sorts of greens.
I'm taking control, and I'm serious.
Come harvest, we'll all be delirious.
We'll have hundreds of donuts coming out of the ground,
'cause I planted a whole box of Cheerios!

Kids

I took the last cookie. It was happier with me.
And I switched off his show and put mine on TV.
I played with his truck, though it made him real mad,
and I spilled a few secrets to make him look bad.
I hid his right shoe, threw his clothes on the lawn,
drew a cat on his homework,
and his baseball glove's gone.
Got ahold of his laptop and erased a few vids—
Then he DARED to talk mean to me!

Some people's kids!

The Know-It-All

I can show in Roman numerals my birthday and my age.
I know why the sky looks blue and what a noun is.
I know all about George Washington and the seasons of the year.
On a map, I'll even show you where my town is.
I know some long division and the phases of the moon,
and just why the leaves on autumn trees will blow off.
So I won't be going back to school. I already know it all,
and it's really not polite to be a show-off.

Shirt

I'm sorry, red and purple shirt.
You've always been my favorite.
We had some great adventures,
and each time I'd stop and savor it.
I wore you to my cousin's,
I wore you to the mall.
I wore you to some parties and
sometimes when I played ball.
I wore you twice to church
and to the beach and on vacation.
But now it seems you've gone and changed,
and left me with frustration.
I tried to put you on today,
but you just wouldn't permit me.
Why can't we be the way we were,
way back when you still fit me?

Recycled

My mom's big on recycling.
She wants everything reused.
So I do my share to make
this household green.
Like today I took the Kleenex
from that time I had my cold,
and I tossed it in the laundry
to get clean.

Stuffed

About fifty stuffed animals live on my bed,
dogs, cats and teddy bears, too.
Plus some bunnies & horses & foxes & mice,
and their grandpa, a green kangaroo.
They play with each other, get married, have kids,
go for rides in a shoebox and more.
And they all sleep with pillows
and blankets each night.
As for me, I just sleep on the floor.

Dinner

McNuggetts, and hot dogs, a hot mac & cheese,
some pizza, spaghetti and fries.
These six major food groups are all a kid needs.
Whoever says something else lies.
So don't hand me a menu when we go out to eat
full of Mexican, Chinese and Thai.
Just take the six basics and mix 'em together,
then pass me that chocolate cream pie.

Skeeters

I do not like mosquitoes.
Prob'ly no one does.
They have no right to bite me
or annoy me with their buzz.
But they all will be astonished
the next time they attack.
I'm finished being the victim.
Next time, I'll bite them back.

Present

I'm told it's a marvelous present,
and expensive as well, they said.
They said I was lucky to have one,
and to not let it go to my head.
Ev'ryone at the party was jealous.
Ev'ry boy wished the present was his.
Now they're gone and I sit here just staring,
trying to guess what the stupid thing is.

Window

My baseball broke a window, Mom.
It was sent there by my bat.
I told it twice to stop, but
baseballs often won't do that.
There has to be some punishment,
some kind of penalty.
Please ground them for a week (that is,
the ball and bat, not me).

Good Night

Good night, North Star outside my bedroom window,
and thanks for watching over me tonight.
I'm sure that all is well when you're on duty,
as above the neighbors' roof you shine so bright.
And, sure, sometimes you get a little chilly,
pulling up some blanket clouds to keep you warm.
But I know you're up there anyway, like always,
so, till day, let's keep each other from all harm.

Driver

Mom? Dad? I'm taking the car.
Could one of you toss me the keys?
I won't be gone long and I won't go too far.
I'll even buy gas, if you please.
I know I'm just seven, going on eight,
but I've learned how to do it, from you.
You just slam down the gas and then
stomp on the brake,
and then run through a red light or two.
And if anyone's slow you just
zoom on around them.
At those silly red signs, never stop.
Then you chat now and then with that
man from the car with the
flashing blue lights on the top!

Creativity

I agree. I should pick up my stuff off the floor.
Clutter just isn't very appealing.
So I picked up my stuff, got some glue and behold!
Now it's all neatly stuck to the ceiling!

Allowance

I get a small allowance. It isn't very much.
It's just my pay for doing all my daily chores and such.
But of course there are deductions
before I get my share.
Dad says this is the way that grown-ups do it ev'rywhere.
It's ten percent for breakfast, fifteen percent for lunch,
another twelve percent for all the snacks I sometimes munch.
Then twenty for my housing, and seven for my clothes.
The TV tax is high, but I can't miss my favorite shows.
Plus there's a fee for water, electricity and toys,
and a penalty for waking baby up with all my noise.
All in all, I'm glad to get it. It's an honor, so to speak.
And I only end up owing fifty-seven cents a week!

Burned

Sunburn. I hate it.
All I did was go and play
in the happy, healthy sunshine
of a lovely summer day,
and I came back home on fire
from my forehead to my heels.
Now I know just how a burger
on some glowing charcoal feels.
So tonight we'll have a campfire,
and I'm showing up prepared,
with a helmet, gloves and parka.
You will not see my skin bared.
It will, of course, be awkward
when we do the songs and dances,
but I don't know if there's "moonburn,"
and I ain't takin' chances.

Dark

I'm never afraid of the dark now.
Gave that up when I was three,
'cause I learned a powerful secret:
dark's afraid of me.
For whenever I enter a room now,
where the darkness likes to stay,
by simply flipping the wall switch
I make darkness run away!

Thief

Bunnies simply don't lay eggs.
He must've took 'em from a bird.
So my Easter basket's full of stolen property.
And that makes me an accomplice.
Soon the cops will track me down,
while he escapes Scot-free, all hippy-hoppity
He's the Easter Bunny thief.
He's been doing this for years,
Why we celebrate his crime spree is most curious.
Kids like me will go to jail
thanks to Peter Cottontail.
(If it wasn't for the chocolate, I'd be furious.)

Tree

I've never climbed a tree before.
I bet it's lots of fun.
I bet up there you can look around
and see most everyone,
and hear the leaves all rustling,
and feel wind toss your hair,
and ride a bouncing tree limb.
I bet it's great up there.
The maple in our back yard
looks bigger than our house.
Bet a kid could scamper up there
just as quick as any mouse.
A kid like that's a hero,
never giving in to fear.
So give it all you've got, my friend!
I think I'll wait down here.

Bicycle

Today I will ride this bike.
I know. I've said that before.
I've seen a thousand kids do it.
It can't be too much of a chore.
I'm far too grown up to need training wheels.
I want to know how bike freedom feels.
But I've bruised both my elbows,
my knees, my heels
and crashed into each post and tree.
Now I just need to find
a clear view, a sharp mind,
and a sidewalk with no gravity.

The Last

Why am I always the last to be picked
whenever the kids choose up sides?
There goes Tommy and Austin and Corey and Mick,
yet I wait with the lost cast-asides.
I'm prepared to be just what they want. I am wearing
one ice skate, one baseball cleat, shoulder pads, too,
one bicycle helmet, and I'm brave, bold and daring,
my soccer ball's white and my hackeysack's blue.
I can be a great shortstop or point guard or goalie.
Hurry! Choose me before the game starts!
But they all point and laugh at me. How could I know
that the game we were playing was darts?

Cleaning

So she told me to clean up my room. She did.
And I worked very hard on it. I'm a good kid.
I grabbed rake and shovel to see what was hid
in the clutter and stuff on my floor.
I found some old posters and seven lost socks,
five T-shirts, some pizza and twelve kinds of rocks,
a gift I bought Mom last year, wrapped in its box,
and a vid-game I lost at age four.
There were all kinds of papers and pieces of wood
and Styrofoam peanuts that didn't taste so good,
and dead worms in a box that in all likelihood
I had bought when I fished with my Dad.
But the deeper I dug, more surprises I found,
little treasures from childhood buried around.
But the best little treasure, about three feet down,
was a brother I didn't know I had.

Pets

"Sure," I said, "I'll take care of the family pets.
"Not a prob. I've seen lots of kids do it."
So my folks went to dinner with no big regrets,
and I figured there wasn't much to it.
Soon I thought it was time to take pets for a walk,
but I couldn't find no leashes to hold 'em.
Still I wouldn't let that be my stumbling block,
I used string so they'd do what I told 'em.
Then away we did go, just the pets, strings and me.
Got as far down as Adam and Trish's.
But this whole walking thing I discovered, you see,
doesn't work well with tropical fishes.

Downscaling

Can I get a bronco, a bronco, a bronco?
They're telling me no. Our apartment won't fit him.
Then can I get a pony, a pony, a pony?
Again they said no, though I swore I wouldn't hit him.
How 'bout a Great Dane, a Great Dane, a Great Dane?
No again. Seems no dogs are allowed where we're living
Then a kitty, a kitty, a kitty for me?
Sorry. Sis is allergic, and not too forgiving.
Then one little bunny, a bunny, a bunny?
Too messy, they say. My folks can't abide 'em.
So we're getting a hamster, a hamster, a hamster.
Now I just have to learn how to ride him.

Smile

We call it a smile moon at my house.
It looks like a big backwards C.
And when I go to sleep and it's there in my window,
I imagine God smiling at me.

Tables

Thanksgiving again. All the family's here,
Uncle Joe, Cousin Grace and Aunt Mabel,
plus another two dozen whose names I don't know,
and they all crowd around the big table.
But I don't get to sit there.
I really wouldn't fit there.
I'm considered just a kid there, and so
it's the little card table for me and a few
of the younger Whose Names I Don't Know.
I imagine someday I'll sit up near the turkey
(if a turkey it is. I can't see it).
Then my kids will sit 24 feet away
and complain, but I'll simply decree it.
They'll say it's not fair, sticking them way down there
in such mean and insulting positions.
But what can I say? It is Thanksgiving Day,
when we honor our family traditions.

Brown and Blue

My Aunt Josie doesn't know me or my older brother either.
We're "the kids" to her, not persons of our own.
She doesn't know our ages or our hobbies or our tastes.
When she visits, she "prefers to be alone."
Christmas comes and ev'ry gift from her will be a pair of something,
one in brown and one in blue. It doesn't matter
if it's shirts or trucks or sweaters, baseball caps or pens or bikes,
one in brown and one in blue, and we smile at her.
But look. My hair is yellow and my brother's hair is brown,
he wears glasses and I'm at least six inches shorter.
You would think she'd see the difference. We're not two of a kind.
One more detail: he's a son and I'm a daughter.

Birthday

My brother's two years older but I'll catch up. Don't you worry.
My birthday's in November and his in January.
Each December I get closer, then fall back right after New Year's.
I get close, one year between us. Then zap! it's back to two years.
It seems unfair. I gain some ground, but one way or another
I always lose, and I'm fed up with being little brother.
So here's my plan to knock him off his "I'm the oldest" throne:
I'm going to steal his birthdays and then use them as my own.
I'll take his birthday cake, scrape his name off of the icing,
and substitute my own name, which I'm sure he'll find surprising.
I'll open all his birthday gifts and send each thank-you note.
Then folks will think it's my day, (ha!) and I'll just sit and gloat.
In no time, I'm the older kid and he's just my kid brother.
I'll make things like they ought to be…one way or another.

Shower

Okay! I'll take a shower!
I'll stay there for an hour!
Rapunzel in her tower
won't have hair as clean as mine.
And I'll scrub each inch of skin,
each elbow, knee and shin,
plus my feet, my neck, my chin.
Ev'ry bit of me will shine.
But it's just cuz I agreed to.
I really do not need to.
You know what this could lead to?
Taking showers ev'ry day!
Mom's trying to pull a fast one.
Did she forget my past one?
She knows I took my last one
just a year ago last May!

Afraid

When a kid's afraid of spiders,
when a kid's afraid of storms,
some adult will come and put an arm around him.
When a kid's afraid of dentists
or of heights or of the dark,
it's for sure that love and care will soon surround him.

But all I get is laughed at.
No one gently comforts me
'cause the things that scare me don't scare other kids.
I'm afraid of things like Jello
and dandelions and clouds
and especially those yogurt cups with lids.

So I'm starting to suspect that
an official list exists
of things a kid's allowed to be afraid of.
And mine didn't make the cut,
so I won't be getting hugged.
Guess I'm made of stuff the other kids aren't made of.

Candy Plan

It's tough being sick on a Halloween night,
and not to go out trick or treating.
Mom says getting well is my only concern,
and not all that bad candy eating.
But I'll sit in my house's front window
with a flashlight lit under my chin,
and whenever the kids come to knock on our door
I'll howl with a mad demon's grin.
I figure I'll scare all the children away,
before Mom can distribute our treats.
By the end of the night, I'll just keep them as mine.
Y'know, none of the work, all the sweets.

Polite

Aunt Millie offers cookies.
Mom says, "Just take a few."
My cousin offers candy.
Mom says, "Just one or two."
So when in church that money plate
is passed, I know what's right.
I only take a couple of bucks.
Mom likes when I'm polite.

Worry

We've had a backyard pool now for at least a couple of years.
I've never gotten in. Don't want to rush it.
'Cause my nasty old big brother says the minute that I do,
he'll push the secret lever down and flush it.

Lawn

The mower is broken, the grass is too tall,
but I know what to do.
You want the lawn just one inch high?
I've got a plan for you.
I took my trusty ruler and a scissors
from the drawer.
Now it's measure each blade and precisely cut.
Should be done in three days or four.

Spider

There's a spider in my bedroom!
Call the cops! Call the Marines!
There's a spider in my bedroom
big as any that I've seen!
Someone squish it! Someone spray it!
Someone smack it with a shoe!
Someone kill it 'fore it spins a web,
'cause that's what spiders do!
If it bites me on the ankle,
I could wind up dead or blind!
Wait! It's black fuzz from the laundry?
Well... ...in that case, never mind.

Tears

The clouds held a family reunion
this evening right over my town.
And they're oh so delighted
to get back together,
their tears of joy keep falling down.

Runaway

That's it! I've had enough!
I will run away from home.
I will show my mom who's boss now.
'Cross the countryside I'll roam.
I will wander hills and valleys!
I'll swim rivers, lakes and streams!
I will climb the highest mountains
as I chase my dearest dreams!
I will run away from home now,
my true destiny to meet!
(But first I have to ask my mom
to help me cross the street.)

Boom

July the Fourth we celebrate
how we beat the English king,
and started up the USA
to let our freedoms ring.
But I'm not sure how we did it.
From all that I can tell,
we should have quickly lost that war,
and lost it bad as well.
I mean, the British army had
a lot of guns and swords,
and cannons that went boom! and stuff,
and all we could afford
were fireworks, sparklers, glow sticks,
firecrackers by the ton.
We were so outmatched in weapons,
it's amazing that we won.

Death

What is dying like? I asked grampa if he knows.
He just smiled and said, "Go bring me that big box of Cheerios."
So I did and he scribbled on it with a big, black marker pen.
"What is it now?" he asked me, and I was puzzled then.
"It's still a box of Cheerios," I told him. He said, "Right."
then he smashed the box's corner on the floor with all his might.
"What is it now?" he asked me of the battered, scribbled wreck.
"It's still a box of Cheerios," I said. He said, "Correct!"
Then he tore a bit of corner off and softly said, "What now?"
I didn't know what to say except, "It's Cheerios anyhow!"
With a gentle smile he opened it and took out the bag inside.
The box was in his left hand, the bag was in his right.
"This is all that death is. My dear, we leave our box,
"but we're still God's bag of Cheerios."

Me and grampa have great talks.

Sweet Tooth

The Tooth Fairy gives me a buck for each tooth
she finds under my pillow at night.
And I do like the money, but to tell you the truth,
the whole process just makes me uptight.
'Cause I don't have a lot more to offer,
but she's old and might fall for a bluff.
So I've started to leave her white Tic Tacs,
Twenty bucks, and I'll call it enough.

Car

We traded in our old car.
Got another in its place.
It hasn't said its name yet.
I can't recognize its face.
It wasn't there on my first school day,
or the day I won the game.
It wasn't ours when my sis got born,
or our new pup homeward came.
We drove to Colorado
in the old one, not the new,
and when thunder boomed over our backyard camp,
to its safe embrace we flew.
I remember fake snowflakes and streamers
we stuck on for the Christmas parade.
The new one doesn't know any of that.
It's a stranger, I'm afraid.
Still I hate to think it's lonely
sitting out there clean and strong.
So I baptized the thing with my chocolate milk.
Now it feels like it belongs.

The School
Life Poems

Welcome

Welcome to our school. Welcome to our world.
Welcome to our place of fun and trials.
Welcome to the place where teachers push us to succeed
just as long as we're in quiet, single files.
Though we prob'ly won't admit it,
we love every day we're here
and we love the folks who shape us every day.
It's our place of friends and challenges,
our crazy other home,
and we wouldn't have it any other way.

My Locker

I know I have a locker.
I have a lock and all.
But every now and then it
disappears from down the hall.
We met when school started,
got along about a week.
But then I heard it giggle.
Now it's playing hide and seek.
Whenever I don't need it,
like when parents' night comes round,
oh sure, it's standing proudly
in its place, glad to be found.
But when I've got three minutes
between science class and math,
I race in vain to watch it
gaily skipping down the path.
I do not like my locker.
I know it likes its fun.
But one of us must leave this school
some day. Hope I'm the one.

The Substitute

Substitute teacher, can I get a drink?
Can I sharpen my pencil
and wash up at the sink?
Have you found our class hamster?
Will a ponytail burn?
When we came in from recess,
why didn't Robert return?
Could you spare a large Band-Aid?
I ate paint. Will I die?
There, there, substitute teacher.
No reason to cry.

Names

I think I've learned each name in class.
C'mon, challenge me. I'm sure I'll pass.
There's Barry and Cary and Larry and Terry
and Mary and Sherry and Jerry and Harry.
There's Dina and Lena and Gina and Nina
and Jane.
And just to make it easier,
my best friend will be Jane.
I know that that's the coward's way.
But it's that, or burst my brain.

Johnny Quiller

It isn't right to pick on kids
because of how they look.
What we call weird, to someone else
is normal in their book.
So never mock a classmate.
Let sweet tolerance prevail.
And don't laugh at Johnny Quiller
just because he has a tail.

To the Point

I have hated wearing braces since the moment they went on,
and I feel that "weirdo" on my face is stenciled.
But the other kids are happy. They like having me around,
'cause they use my mouth for sharpening their pencils.

Love

I think I'm in love with that new boy in my class.
He's so handsome, smart and clever. Really hot.
He starts next week and, no, I haven't seen or met him yet,
but he must be better than the boys we've got.

Allegiance

We all pledge allegiance to the red, white and blue.
We do it together each day.
I have no idea what "allegiance" means,
but it seems like a nice thing to say.
Something to do with some legions, I think,
or leashes or leases or leeches.
But if they prevent us from starting our work,
I'm in favor of all kinds of speeches.

Answer

No! Look over here! I'm waving my hand!
I've raised it as high as I possibly can.
I bounce up and down, trying to get you to pick me.
This answer I know! Let me spit it out quickly!
I'll dazzle my classmates! Make an awesome impression!
But first tell me one thing: what again was the question?

Find X

Numbers for angles, numbers for lines,
numbers for length, depth and height.
Then letters for this and more letters for that,
and then diagrams. Oh, what a sight!
And it's always the same. "Find X" we are told,
from somewhere inside the whole mess.
But if it always gets lost,
couldn't we just pass the hat
and go buy X a good GPS?

Rain

We can't play outside today just 'cause it's raining.
They simply announce it. No word of explaining.
But grown-ups confuse me. They let us take showers,
and run through the sprinklers for hours and hours,
and dive into pools and get soaked by balloons,
and swim in the rivers and lakes and lagoons.
But somehow on school days, all this they forget,
and say, "Don't play outside 'cause you'll get yourself wet."

In Line

Stand in line for the washroom.
Stand in line for your food.
Stand in line for the school bus.
No cuts, 'cause that'd be rude.
Stand in line for a fire drill.
Keep standing in line, teacher said.
But she never did say we should stand on our feet,
so I usually stand on my head.

Late

I'm sorry my report is late.
I wrote it Thursday night at eight,
and every word was really great
but then disaster struck.
My baby brother tore it up,
and gave page three to our darling pup,
then Mommy spilled her coffee cup
and I was out of luck.
So I rushed to print it out anew,
but the whole computer mainframe blew.
and the hard drive did what hard drives do:
it crashed like a crystal glass.
And then—excuse me? What'd you say?
Is any of this true? No way!
Why should that matter anyway
in creative writing class?

Baloney and Cheese

Baloney and cheese, baloney and cheese.
Couldn't I have something that's different, please?
Day after day of this stuff gets depressing!
Couldn't I have turkey with stuffing and dressing?
Couldn't I get brownies still warm and inviting?
Baloney and cheese just is not that exciting.
Isn't there anything else you could stir up,
Like maybe some waffles with blueberry syrup?
A big plate of pasta or cheese ravioli,
burritos and tacos with fresh guacamole,
Some barbecue chicken, some nachos con queso,
the stuff that you know makes my mouth hip-hooray so
An extra-large pizza with hot pepperoni!

But it's eat this or starve, I guess.
Good ol' baloney.

Rope Climber

Yesterday my coach said, "Climb that rope,"
and climb that rope I did.
Soon I hope he'll tell me, "Come on down."
I'm a very obedient kid.

Frances

My name is Frances Fisher. All my teachers like me best
That's why they put my initials at the top of all my tests.

Independent Thought

When they tell us to go, we go.
When they tell us to stop, we stop.
When they tell us to stand, we stand.
When they tell us to sit, we drop.
When they tell us to speak, we speak.
When they say, "Show your homework," it's shown.
Then they ask, in the depths of the teachers' lounge,
"Why can't these kids think on their own?"

Principal

To the principal's office again I am sent
for the twentieth time of the year.
We're getting to know each other quite well,
'cause my teacher keeps sending me here.
She says I'm disruptive and loud and a pain,
but she don't see my system, I guess.
I only act naughty on Tuesdays at ten,
to get out of arithmetic tests.

Sweet

Our chess is club is recruiting.
We need new members bad.
So here's our secret plan. Please don't repeat it.
In games now, when you take a piece,
it's made of chocolate,
and you get to bite his head clean off and eat it!

Alarming

Look. I've heard if we only stare long enough at it,
the fire alarm will go off.
We must focus and concentrate, each one together.
Do not blink, do not speak, do not cough.
It is crucial that all of us trust in our powers
We cannot leave room for a doubt.
I believe we can do this, but we must do it now—
he's handing the test papers out!

Aardvark

I'm changing my name to Aardvark.
Abraham Aardvark. Count on it.
Then every report card I get from now on
will have at least six A's upon it.

Super Student

Oh, I love to learn arithmetic.
I delight in science tests.
Pop quiz in history? That's my fun,
but those ACTs are best.
I can hardly wait for report cards.
I view homework as a treat.
Now my parents say
there's a kind and friendly
doctor I should meet.

The Loop

I'm sorry. I'm terribly shaken. Upset.
My emotions can't deal with this news.
I'm sweating. I'm pacing. I worry. I fret.
I'm trembling down to my shoes.
Mrs. Johnson just told me she once was a student here!
Sat in these chairs! Ran this race!
Now she's back as a teacher.
She's caught in a loop!
Is there no getting out of this place?

Historical First

This last weekend it was my turn to
take home the classroom pet.
a big rabbit by the name of Cheerio.
And by accident, I let him out
and too close he did get
to our family cookout on the patio.
And it just was not my fault that
my grilled frankfurter he grabbed
and he scarfed it down just like he was a hog.
But I'm pretty sure that I'm the first kid in all history
who can truly say my homework ate my dog.

Detention

A detention? For me? Oh, how sweet, Mrs. Blair.
Getting presents is always such fun.
But I'm sorry. I can't. I've had more than my share
and there are so many kids who've had none.
Being greedy is wrong, my sweet mother explained,
and she certainly has a point there.
So I'll have to decline this one. Please don't be pained.
Try me later. Okay, Mrs. Blair?

Small

My bookbag kept on breaking
so I used my shrinking ray.
Now I carry them all in a Zip-Loc bag
and I can't read what they say.

Yay!

We have the greatest cheerleaders.
They dance and bounce and yell,
build pyramids and leap about
and toss the girls so well
With them and our great pom-pon squad,
they make everybody scream.
And I hope and pray that someday soon
we'll start a football team.

Belief

I don't believe in studying,
or in doing homework neither.
So you'd violate my new beliefs
to expect me to do either.
And kids can join my brand-new church
without a fee or dunking.
We pray each day for the miracle
that will keep us all from flunking.

Lost

School bus, school bus in a line
bright and yellow. Which is mine?
Makes no difference. Just sit down.
So many pretty streets in town!

Traded

When I joined my school's football team,
I was proud they made me captain.
I was sure we'd be the champs, but
no one told me this could happen.
'Bout an hour ago, the coach said,
"Son, excuse my being blunter.
"You've been traded to another school
"for a center and a punter."
Now my family has to pack and move us
to some town called New Briar.
They take football far too serious here.
Think I should've joined the choir.

Report Card

I'm writing my teacher's report card.
I'm giving her grades for her work.
I'll try not to be too demanding or harsh
'cause I don't want to seem like a jerk.
But she does need to know we don't get enough play,
and the homework must end, and the tests go away.
But it looks like she'll never advance her career:
she's been stuck in fifth grade for six years.

Lonely

Do schools all get lonely when the children go home?
Do they miss all the noise and the chatter?
Does it make them feel sad when they're left all alone,
and on weekends do they get even sadder?
Oh, school, we still love you. The feeling still glows.
Very soon it's to you we'll be bound.
And you're never abandoned, 'cause ev'ry kid knows
that the teachers live there all year round!

THE FINALE

The Band

(strictly to a 2/4 tempo)

We're the band! (boom, tweet)
We're the band! (bleat, squeak)
playing music we don't really understand (morg, zeep)
We can really draw a crowd when we play it nice and loud
and it makes our parents proud that
we're the band! (brat, beep)

We're the band! (brawp, fleep)
We're the band! (thoomp, pleep)
and our uniforms look positively grand! (crunk, greep)
We play classical and pop, Sousa marches and be-bop,
till they all beg us to stop.
We're the band! (flork, threep)

We're the band! (hornk, squeep)
We're the band! (spronk, preep)
Our conductor covers his ears with both his hands! (lorp, sneep)
We play tunes in C and G but we seldom can agree.
Some play in F, some play in B, but
We're the band! (tormp, dreep)

We're the band! (frorg, gleep)
We're the band! (snirp, kleep)
Out of step and out of tune, but in demand (hork, queep)
Whether simple or complex,
we turn all our tunes to wrecks,
and we're comin' to your street next!
We're the band! (thormp, meep)

ABOUT THE AUTHOR

Brian is retired and lives in Frankfort, IL. He is known as a singer, songwriter, playwright, actor, director and musician, and has spent 40 years performing at Renaissance fairs throughout the country as "Tinker MacLea." He appears on some 24 albums of his music, but this is his first effort as a writer of books for children.

www.ingramcontent.com/pod-product-compliance
Lightning Source LLC
Chambersburg PA
CBHW022145060526
44654CB00043B/676